Our Bodies

How Does My Body Work?

Charlotte Guillain

raintree

Schools Library and Information Services

Raintree is an imprint of Capstone Global Library Limited, a company incorporated in England and Wales having its registered office at 7 Pilgrim Street, London, EC4V 6LB – Registered company number: 6695582

Edited by Daniel Nunn, Rebecca Rissman, and Harriet Milles
Designed by Joanna Hinton-Malivoire
Picture research by Mica Brancic
Illustrations © Capstone Global Library Ltd.
Originated by Capstone Global Library Ltd.
Production by Eirian Griffiths
Printed and bound in China by Leo Paper Products Ltd

ISBN 978 1 406 22895 3 (hardback)
15 14 13 12 11
10 9 8 7 6 5 4 3 2 1

ISBN 978 1406 22965 3 (paperback)
20 19 18 17 16 15
10 9 8 7 6 5 4

British Library Cataloguing in Publication Data
Guillian, Charlotte.
    How does your body work?. – (Acorn plus)
    1. Human body–Pictorial works–Juvenile literature.
    2. Human physiology–Pictorial works–Juvenile literature. 3. Human anatomy–Pictorial works–Juvenile literature.
    I. Title II. Series
    612-dc22
A full catalogue record for this book is available from the British Library.

Acknowledgements
We would like to thank the following for permission to reproduce photographs: © Capstone Global Library **p. 17** (Karon Dubke); Corbis **p. 5** (© Joson); iStockphoto **pp. 4, 21 left** (© Jacek Chabraszewski), **6 left** (© Rosemarie Gearhart), **7** (© temet), **8** (© Cliff Parnell), **10** (© Marzanna Syncerz), **12** (© Aldo Murillo), **13** (© Ivan Ivanov), **15** (© Suzanne Tucker), **16** (© Zhang Bo), **19 right** (© Robert Churchill), **20** (© Mandygodbehear), **21 right** (© Jesse Kunerth); Science Photo Library **p. 11** (© Gustoimages); Shutterstock **pp. 9** (© Kamira), **14** (© Darren Whitt), **18** (© PHOTOCREO Michal Bednarek).

Front cover photograph of a girl doing a handstand in a park reproduced with permission of Photolibrary (Tetra Images/PT Images). Back cover photograph of a grazed knee reproduced with permission of iStockphoto (© Suzanne Tucker).

We would like to thank Dr. Matt Siegel for his invaluable help in the preparation of this book.

Every effort has been made to contact copyright holders of any material reproduced in this book. Any omissions will be rectified in subsequent printings if notice is given to the publisher.

Contents

Some words appear in bold, **like this**. You can find out what they mean in "Words to know" on page 23.

Outside your body

face

hand

foot

Your body is made of many different parts. You can see some parts of your body on the outside. Your arms, legs, hands, feet, and face are on the outside of your body.

skin

Your **skin** is on the outside of your body. Skin protects the inside of your body. It can stop you getting too hot or too cold. Skin can mend itself if you get a cut.

Your bones

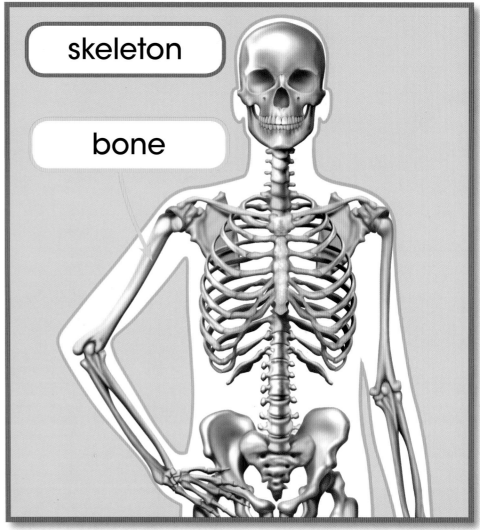

skeleton

bone

You have **bones** all over your body. Bones make up your **skeleton**. Your skeleton holds your body up.

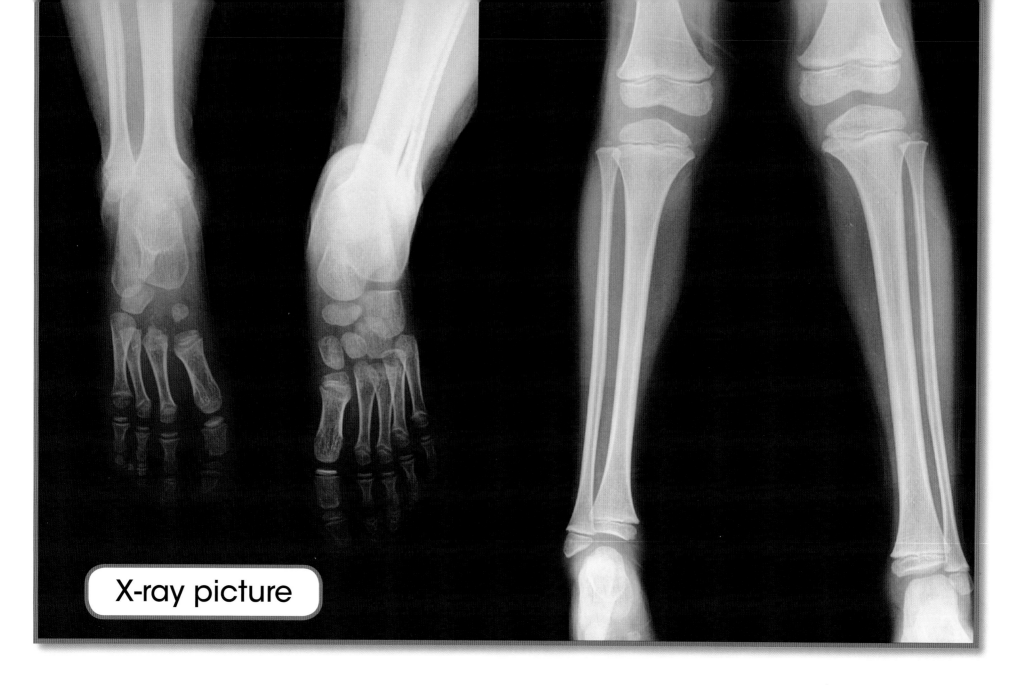

X-ray picture

Your bones are very hard and strong. Some bones are big and some bones are small. You can see your bones in an **X-ray** picture.

Your brain

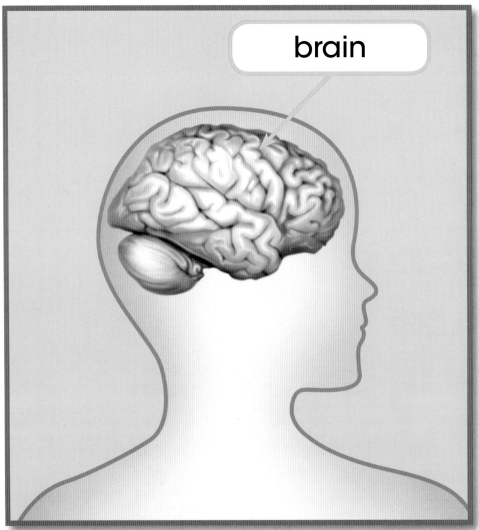

brain

Your **brain** is inside your head. Your brain controls your body. The **bones** in your head keep your brain safe.

You learn, remember, and feel things with your brain. Your brain tells you if you are happy, sad, hot, cold, or feeling pain.

Your lungs

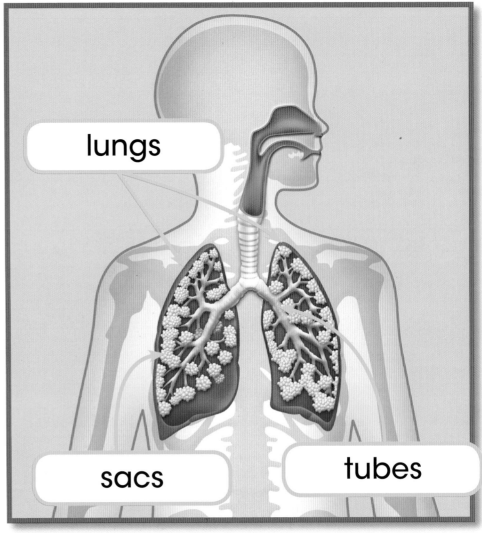

lungs

sacs

tubes

You breathe with your **lungs**. There are two soft lungs inside your chest. **Bones** called ribs keep your lungs safe. Your lungs are made of **tubes** and little pockets, called sacs.

Your lungs breathe in the air you need to live. You can feel your chest move as you breathe in and out. You breathe slowly when you are still. You breathe faster when you run.

Your heart and blood

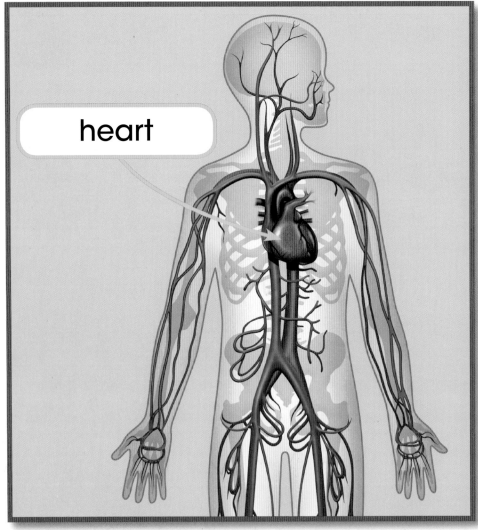

heart

Your **heart** is inside your chest. It is about the size of your **fist**. Your heart is made of **muscle**, with **tubes** coming out of it. Your heart **pumps blood** through the tubes.

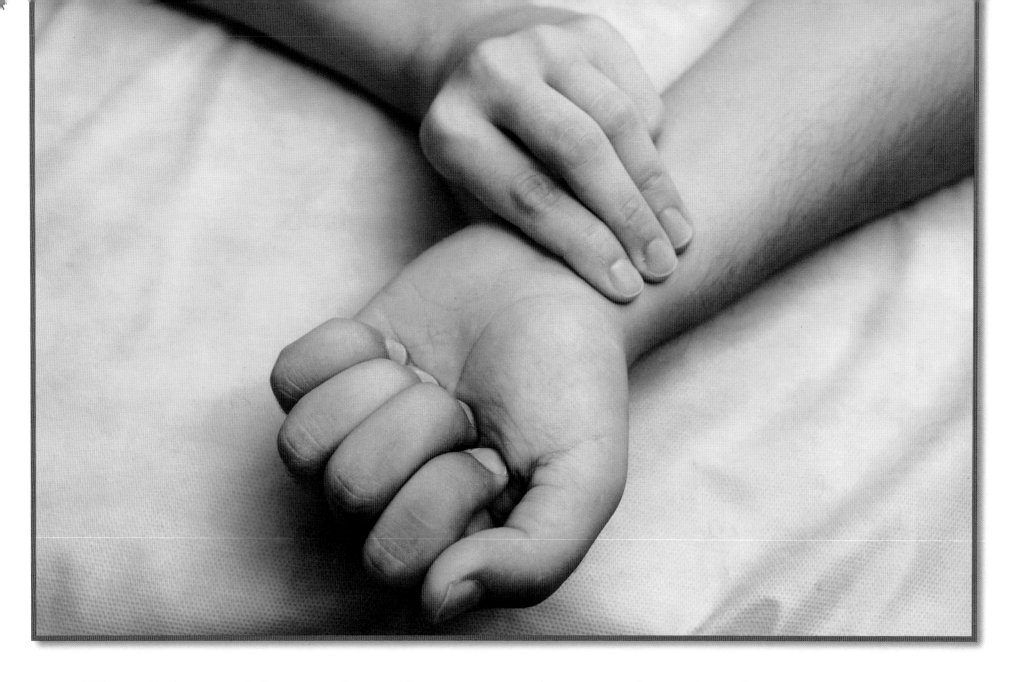

The blood travels all around your body. As your heart pumps, you can feel it beat. Your heart beats slowly when you are still. It beats fast when you run.

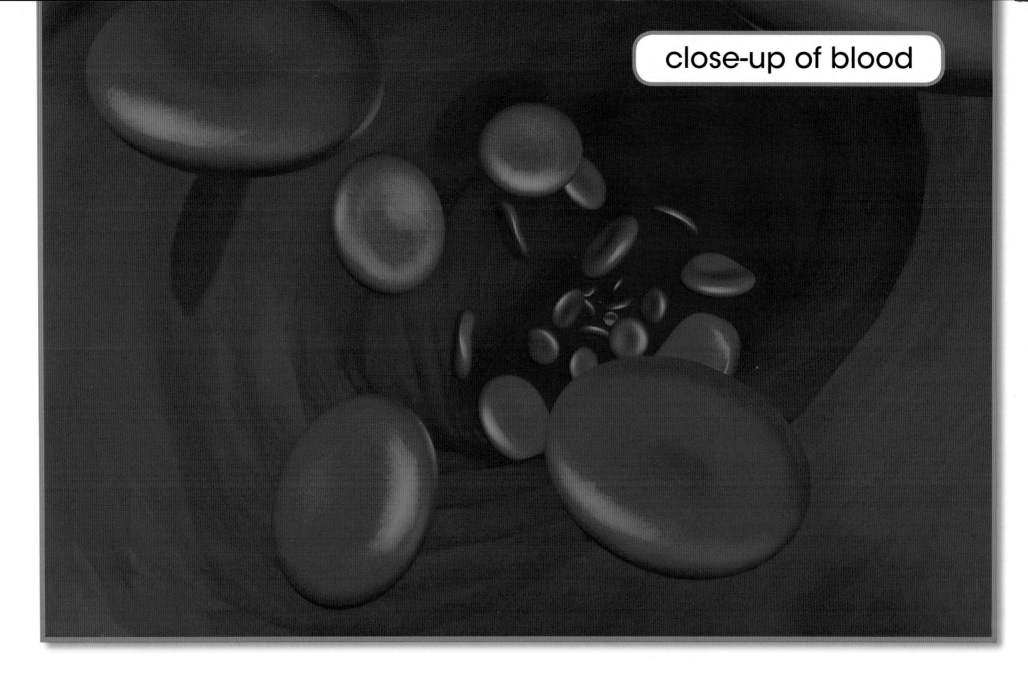

close-up of blood

Blood is wet and red. Blood travels around your body. Blood carries the things your body needs to live, such as food and **oxygen**.

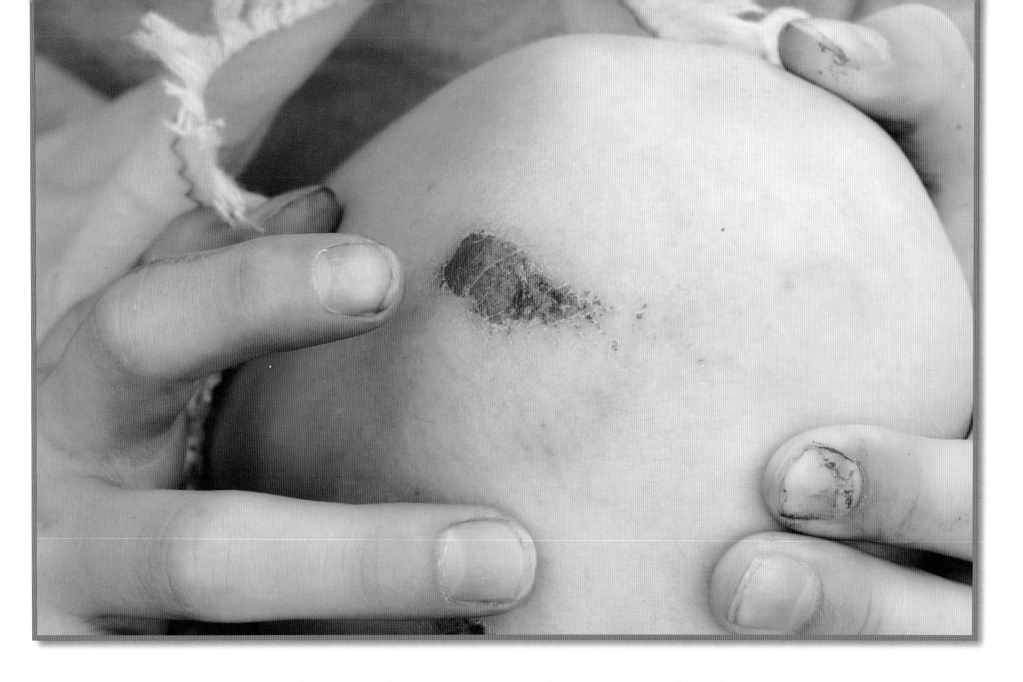

You can see blood if you cut yourself. Then a
scab will form on your **skin**. The scab will stop
your bleeding and help to heal the cut.

Your stomach

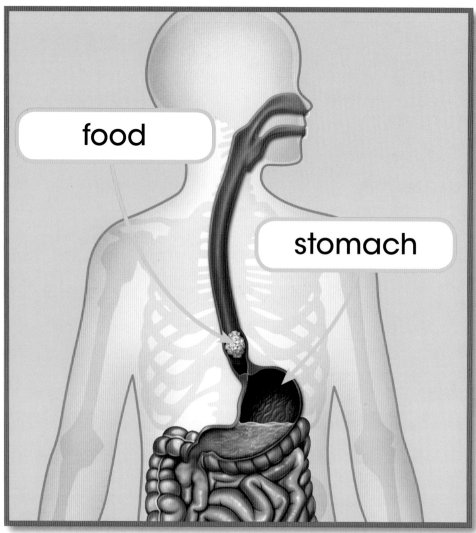

food

stomach

Your **stomach** is inside your tummy. Your stomach is like a bag. When you swallow food it goes into your stomach. Your stomach breaks up the food you eat so your body can use it.

Your stomach stretches as it fills up with food. You feel hungry when your stomach is empty. You feel full when you have eaten enough.

Your muscles

You have **muscles** all over your body. Muscles make your body move. Some muscles work without you thinking. They keep your body working properly. Your **heart** works even when you are asleep.

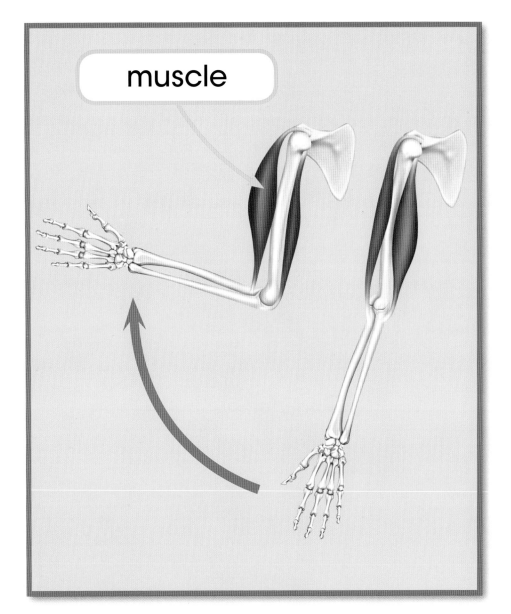

muscle

Some muscles are joined to your **bones**. You choose to move these muscles. You use these muscles to move around. You move your leg muscles when you run or jump.

Keeping your body healthy

It is important to keep your body healthy. Drinking water is good for your whole body. Drinking milk is good for your **bones** and teeth. Eating fruit and vegetables helps your body grow and stay strong.

You should try to be active for an hour every day.
This could be running, swimming, cycling, or playing
games. You also need plenty of sleep so your body
can grow and stay healthy.

Can you remember?

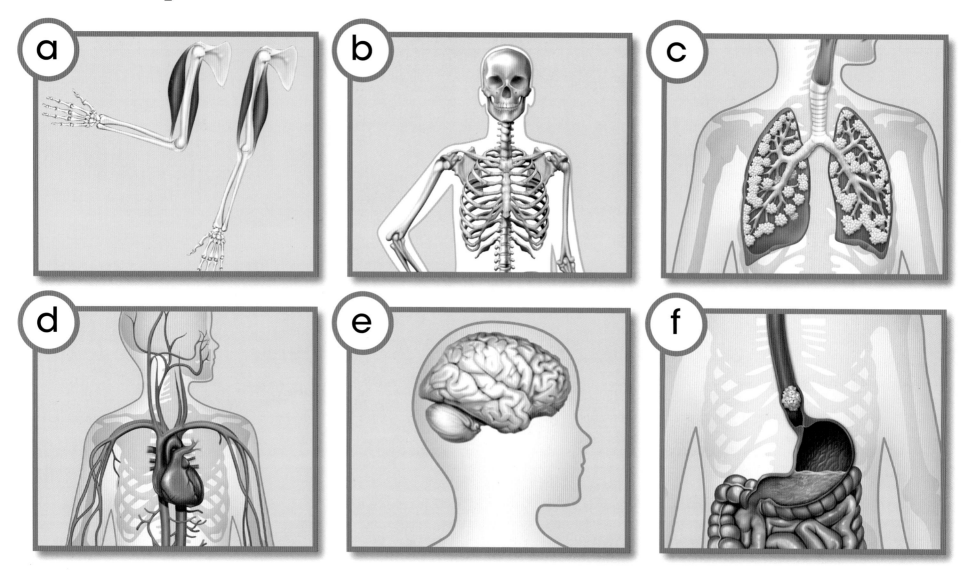

a

b

c

d

e

f

Can you say which parts of your body these pictures are showing?

Answers on page 24

Words to know

blood red liquid inside your body. Blood carries food and air all around your body so it can work.

bone hard part inside your body that holds your body up

brain part of your body inside your head. You think with your brain. Your brain tells your body what to do.

fist clenched hand

heart part of your body inside your chest. Your heart pushes blood around your body.

lung part of your body that helps you breathe. You have two lungs inside your chest.

muscle stretchy part inside your body that can make things move

oxygen part of the air that we need to breathe to stay alive

pump action that forces things up, through, or out of something

scab something your body makes to mend a cut on your skin

skeleton all the bones in a body

skin waterproof layer that covers the outside of your body

stomach part of your body inside your tummy where your food goes

tube long thin pipe, like a hose

X-ray special camera that can see under your skin

Index

Answers to quiz on page 22:
a) muscles b) bones c) lungs d) heart e) brain f) stomach

Notes for parents and teachers

Before reading

Ask the children to name the parts of their body they can see on the outside. Then ask them what parts of their body are inside. Make a list of these together and see if the children know what each body part does, for example, the stomach holds food.

After reading

- Help the children to make "Healthy Body" posters. Ask them to draw a picture of their body with the various body parts discussed and illustrated in the book. Ask them to label each body part and write some tips on the poster on how to keep each part and their whole body healthy. You could put the posters up around the school.

- Ask the children if they can think of ways our bodies change when we exercise. Investigate this with the class by splitting the children into four groups. Explain that everyone will do five minutes of exercise and look for changes in their bodies before and after. One group can observe whether their breathing changes. Another group can investigate whether their heartbeats change. Another group can look out for changes to their skin (they may observe a colour change and sweating). The final group should discuss whether the muscles in their legs feel different before and after exercise. Bring the groups together at the end and discuss what they found out.